This Journal Belongs To

_____

_____

@Copyright 2020 by Laura Thorne

all rights reserved no part of this book may be reproduced or used in any manner without written permission of the copyright owner except for the use of quotations in a book review.

Table Of Content

- About the journal
- How to use the journal
- 12 Fundamentals:
    - Rule of Thirds
    - Depth of Field
    - Framing
    - Cropping
    - Color Contrast
    - Lines
    - Patterns
    - Texture
    - Shadows
    - Reflection
    - perspective
- List of prompts

About The Journal

THE CAPTURE LIFE AS YOU SEE IT JOURNAL IS PERFECT FOR ANYONE NEW TO PHOTOGRAPHY OR THE EXPERIENCED PHOTOGRAPHER WHO JUST WANTS SOME MOTIVATION TO GET OUT THERE AND SHOOT!

This special journal is like no other in that it exists to help you become a better photographer. Each month features a different Fundamental of Photographic Composition plus prompts to join in on weekly missions and other fun suggestions to help keep even the most experienced photographer motivated to keep practicing and learning.

Just about everyone has access to a camera whether they saved up for a fancy DSLR, were handed down a 35 MM, or just have one on their phone. What we don't all have is the basic understanding about how to purposefully craft a photo rather than just take snapshots.

Through practice, you'll have a much keener eye and an ability to see the world as only a skilled photographer can. One of our favorite mottos is #perspectiVechangeseverything as you will see!

Use the weekly summary pages to grab a prompt from the list in the back of the journal, or follow @absolute.reVolution.gallery on Instagram to take part in the weekly group prompt where you can have a chance to get featured or win prizes.

How to use the journal?

Photography is a skill that comes with practice and continuous improvement. In this journal, we've provided a list of fundamentals to learn, a list of prompts to give you a place to start shooting, Something Fun Challenges to get you trying new things, and a community to share with on Instagram @absolute.reVolution.gallery.

Start with focusing on the main theme for the month to learn to recognize the fundamentals of photography. Then use the weekly prompts to practice the fundamental.

Participate in the Something Fun Challenges to stay motivated and get exposure to different types of photography.

Finally, use the blank pages to document what you learn, things you want to explore more, pull ideas out of your head, and talk about how your photography effects how you are feeling on a day to day basis.

Get feedback by sharing and interacting with the others in the @abolute.reVolution.gallery Instagram community using the hashtag:

#absolutereVolutiongallery

Rule Of Thirds

Rule Of Thirds

Most people to try to get the entire subject and place it right in the middle of the shot.

Learning to purposefully arrange the image so that the subject's relationship to the surroundings is seen helps tell a story and is a key difference between a photograph and a snapshot.

Throughout the month, turn the grid setting on your camera or smartphone to "on" and try placing the subject into the different quadrants.

Your images will instantly be more compelling and less repetitive.

Switch between portrait and landscape. One will be better for your composition than the other.

Share with absolute reVolution gallery on Instagram with #absrev_ruleofthirds

Month _____

MONDAY

TUESDAY

WEDNESDAY

THURSDAY

FRIDAY

SATURDAY / SUNDAY

This Week's Prompt

Ideas

Something Fun

DATE: _____

TRY A NEW EDITING APP

Something Fun

DATE: _____

GET OUTSIDE

_____
_____
_____
_____
_____
_____
_____
_____
_____
_____
_____
_____
_____
_____
_____
_____

Something Fun

DATE: _____

GET UP CLOSE TO DETAILS

Depth
Of Field

Depth Of Field

Depth of Field is another essential in photography that separates skilled photography from snapshots.

By focusing on part of the image closer to you and making the background out of focus you help lead the viewer to what you want them to see.

Combining this with rule of thirds can make for some very simple yet dramatic shots.
Try creating depth throughout the month.

To get this effect with your smartphone place the lens close to the subject and hold your finger on the screen.

Share with absolute reVolution gallery
on Instagram with #absrev_depthoffield

Month _____

MONDAY

TUESDAY

WEDNESDAY

THURSDAY

FRIDAY

SATURDAY / SUNDAY

This Week's Prompt

Ideas

Something Fun

DATE: _____

TRY NEW THINGS

_____
_____
_____
_____
_____
_____
_____
_____
_____
_____
_____
_____
_____
_____
_____
_____
_____
_____

Something Fun

DATE: _____

CHANGE YOUR SETTINGS

Something Fun

DATE: _____

SETUP A MINI STUDIO

Framing

Framing is a great way to add intrigue to your images. It gives the viewer they feeling they are getting a sneak peak or behind the scenes secret.

It's not an effect that will always be readily available but once you're looking for it you'll find different ways to get the effect.

You can look through things like windows, doors, archways, hanging tree limbs, or you can try artificially creating a border.

Looking for a frame will help force you to change your perspective. That is, change your physical position.

Share with absolute reVolution gallery
on Instagram with #absrev_framing

Month _____

MONDAY

This Week's Prompt

TUESDAY

WEDNESDAY

Ideas

THURSDAY

FRIDAY

SATURDAY / SUNDAY

Something Fun

DATE: _____

BRING A FRIEND

Something Fun

DATE: _____

MAKE A SET

Something Fun

DATE: _____

TURN FOOD INTO ART

Cropping

Many of us, especially when starting out in photography, tend to try to get the entire subject and place it right in the center of the image.

Counter intuitively, when part of the picture is left out, a bigger story often is told.

By cropping the edges of this flower out, the subject no longer is the flower but the texture, colors, and shadows connecting the center of the flower.

Throughout the month, pay attention to what your subject is and what can you leave out to get more specific about what you want the viewer to see.

Share with absolute reVolution gallery
on Instagram with #absrev_cropping

Month _____

MONDAY

TUESDAY

WEDNESDAY

THURSDAY

FRIDAY

SATURDAY / SUNDAY

This Week's Prompt

Ideas

Something Fun

DATE: _____

USE A FRIEND AS A MODEL

Something Fun

DATE: _____

TRY USING A TRIPOD

_____
_____
_____
_____
_____
_____
_____
_____
_____
_____
_____
_____
_____
_____
_____
_____
_____

Something Fun

DATE: _____

PET PORTRAILS

Color
Contrast

Color Contrast

Contrasting colors are eye catching! You see them in many forms in nature like insects and flower as well as in marketing and signage.

Technically, contrasting colors are opposing colors on the color wheel:
- Orange – Blue
- Yellow – Purple
- Red – Green

Contrast can also be between tones and hues as well.

Throughout the month, seek to create compositions that contain contrasting colors. Easy places to look are in gardens, produce stands, and murals.

Share with absolute reVolution gallery on Instagram with #absrev_colorcontrast

Month _____

MONDAY

_____

TUESDAY

_____

WEDNESDAY

_____

THURSDAY

_____

FRIDAY

_____

SATURDAY / SUNDAY

This Week's Prompt

_____
_____
_____
_____
_____

Ideas

_____
_____
_____
_____
_____
_____
_____
_____

Something Fun

DATE: _____

REVIEW THE COLOR WHEEL

# Something Fun

DATE: _____

USE A NEW FILTER

Something Fun

DATE: _____

WRITE A STORY

_____
_____
_____
_____
_____
_____
_____
_____
_____
_____
_____
_____
_____
_____
_____
_____
_____
_____
_____
_____

Something Fun

DATE: _____

SHARE YOUR FAVE

_____
_____
_____
_____
_____
_____
_____
_____
_____
_____
_____
_____
_____
_____
_____
_____

Lines

Lines are around more than you realize. They can help lead the viewer to a place, draw their attention from one point to another, create emotion and spark interest.

Some of the typical ones are:

- ★ Leading lines – paths, stairs, roads, etc. that start near you and "lead" away from you.
- ★ Contrasting lines – lines that counter act each other – thick vs thin or straight vs crooked.
- ★ S-Curves – lines typical of roads an "S" shape.
- ★ Vanishing points – lines that come together on the horizon.

Throughout the month, keep an eye out for the lines that are all around you!

Share with absolute reVolution gallery on Instagram with #absrev_Lines

Month _____

MONDAY

TUESDAY

WEDNESDAY

THURSDAY

FRIDAY

SATURDAY / SUNDAY

This Week's Prompt

Ideas

Something Fun

DATE: _____

LOOK UP

Something Fun

DATE: _____

GO FOR A HIKE

_____
_____
_____
_____
_____
_____
_____
_____
_____
_____
_____
_____
_____
_____
_____
_____
_____
_____
_____

Something Fun

DATE: _____

START A PROJECT

Patterns

Patterns often build on the concept of lines. Patterns form when lines and shapes create complex and repetitive forms.

Patterns help us make sense of abstract and complex things. In photography, patterns can help dive into details, create order from chaos, and add sense to an image.

Patterns from shapes is often referred to as geometry.

Throughout the month, seek out patterns. When you see something complex, organic, and natural see if you can find a pattern in it all.

Share with absolute reVolution gallery on Instagram with #absrev_patterns

Month _____

MONDAY

TUESDAY

WEDNESDAY

THURSDAY

FRIDAY

SATURDAY / SUNDAY

This Week's Prompt

Ideas

Something Fun

DATE: _____

TRY COLOR POP

_____
_____
_____
_____
_____
_____
_____
_____
_____
_____
_____
_____
_____
_____
_____
_____
_____

Something Fun

DATE: _____

CAPTURE MOVEMENT

Something Fun

DATE: _____

POST A PHOTO STORY

Textures

Texture is that additional layer that can make any image more interesting but it can also stand on its own if you use the fundamentals you've already learned.

Touch is a sensory that attaches to our memories. When you capture the feeling of texture in an image the viewer is able to reach back and attach emotion to your image.

Throughout the month, pay attention to what things are made of, how light brings out or diminishes the surface of an object. See how different angles change the strength of the texture as the subject of the image.

Share with absolute reVolution gallery
on Instagram with #absrev_textures

Month _____

MONDAY

TUESDAY

WEDNESDAY

THURSDAY

FRIDAY

SATURDAY / SUNDAY

This Week's Prompt

Ideas

Something Fun

DATE: _____

FIND A REFLECTION

Something Fun

DATE: _____

GO ON AN ADVENTURE

_____
_____
_____
_____
_____
_____
_____
_____
_____
_____
_____
_____
_____
_____
_____
_____
_____
_____
_____
_____

Something Fun

DATE: _____

CREATE AN ONLINE ALBUM

Reflections

Who doesn't love a good reflection? It's amazing how often we might not see them if we're not looking. Much like shadows, our brains are used to seeing them as natural parts of our surroundings.

Reflections are another way to add depth to your images.

They also inherently add a layer of complexity to the story of the image by invoking a sense of another time, place, or alternative universe.

Spend this month looking for reflections in mirrors, windows, water features, and other surfaces. Try changing your persepctiVe to see how the image changes.

Share with absolute reVolution gallery on Instagram with #absrev_reflections

Month _____

MONDAY

TUESDAY

WEDNESDAY

THURSDAY

FRIDAY

SATURDAY / SUNDAY

This Week's Prompt

Ideas

Something Fun

DATE: _____

TAKE A CLASS

Something Fun

DATE: _____

TAKE AN ABSTRACT

Something Fun

DATE: _____

SET YOUR ALARM & TAKE A PIC

_____
_____
_____
_____
_____
_____
_____
_____
_____
_____
_____
_____
_____
_____
_____
_____

Shadows

Shadows are hidden in plain sight and can open a whole new world to you when you start to see them dancing around.

The best time of day to seek out shadows are in the morning and late afternoon when they are elongated.

Throughout the month, look for the way shadows create lines and extend lines, create abstract patterns, and even anchor a subject in it's spot.

Try focusing on both the object and its shadow as well as the shadow on its own.

Share with absolute reVolution gallery
on Instagram with #absrev_shadows

Month _____

MONDAY

TUESDAY

WEDNESDAY

THURSDAY

FRIDAY

SATURDAY / SUNDAY

This Week's Prompt

Ideas

Something Fun

DATE: _____

MAKE AN INSTAGRAM FRIEND

Something Fun

DATE: _____

MAKE A PINHOLE CAMERA

Something Fun

DATE: _____

EXPERIMENT WITH SHADOWS

Quality
Of Light

Quality Of Light

Quality of light can appear in many ways and can sometimes be so amazing it can serve as the subject itself. Look for light from sunset and sunrise, back lighting, sun rays, diffused light, bounce light, and artificial light.

Light has a direct effect on the mood of an image. Sometimes all you need to do is wait for a cloud to pass or shift position.

Throughout the month, pay attention to how the available light has an effect on the subjects and overall tone of your images. You many need to reposition yourself to get the best effect.

Share with absolute reVolution gallery on Instagram with #absrev_qualityoflight

Month _____

MONDAY

TUESDAY

WEDNESDAY

THURSDAY

FRIDAY

SATURDAY / SUNDAY

This Week's Prompt

Ideas

Something Fun

DATE: _____

ZOOM IN & ZOOM OUT

Something Fun

DATE: _____

CAPTURE SUNRISE & SUNDOWN

_____
_____
_____
_____
_____
_____
_____
_____
_____
_____
_____
_____
_____
_____
_____
_____
_____
_____

Something Fun

DATE: _____

LOOK FOR DECAY

Perspective

PerspectiVe on a high level is how you put you into your photos. All of your experiences and interests make your story telling perspectiVe unique to you.

On the spot, it's whether you are near to, beneath, above, behind, or looking through something. Overtime, you're style will show more of your life perspectiVe.

Throughout the month, use all of the fundamentals you've already learned and also apply your unique perspectiVe. Pay attention to how you position yourself and/or the camera in relation to your subject.

Share with absolute reVolution gallery
on Instagram with #absrev_perspective

Month _____

MONDAY

TUESDAY

WEDNESDAY

THURSDAY

FRIDAY

SATURDAY / SUNDAY

This Week's Prompt

Ideas

Something Fun

DATE: _____

SHARE YOUR YEAR FAVE

_____
_____
_____
_____
_____
_____
_____
_____
_____
_____
_____
_____
_____
_____
_____
_____

Something Fun

DATE: _____

GO ON A SCAVENGERHUNT

Something Fun

DATE: _____

CAPTURE THE SEASON

List Of Prompts

Fuzzy	Grub	Sunshine	Holder
Cielo	Freckles	Good egg	Bestie
Atone	Erased	Reality bites	Hot
Musical	Up and over	Cuisine	Spooky
Too much	Spirit	Weather	Alone
Playful	Love	Line up	Funny
Steady	Travel	Surprise	Blank
Black	Hungry	Big cheese	Green
Casa	Folklore	Joker	Stuffed
Tricked out	Horned	Walk about	Grid
Spades	Neighbor	Feather weight	Stable
Brothers	Sharp	Puppet	Blinky
Pattern	Gracias	Safety dance	Gift

Make sure to follow @absolute.reVolution.gallery on Instagram to see the group weekly prompt

Made in the USA
Las Vegas, NV
23 December 2024